YOUR KNOWLEDGE HAS

Adebayo Omotosho, Kazir Olanrewaju Ganiu, Tosin Adewunmi Ogunkoyode

A survey of e-prescription readiness in selected Nigeria hospitals

GRIN Verlag

Bibliografische Information der Deutschen Nationalbibliothek:

Die Deutsche Bibliothek verzeichnet diese Publikation in der Deutschen National-
bibliografie; detaillierte bibliografische Daten sind im Internet über http://dnb.d-
nb.de/ abrufbar.

Imprint:

Copyright © 2013 GRIN Verlag GmbH
Druck und Bindung: Books on Demand GmbH, Norderstedt Germany
ISBN: 978-3-656-47172-1

This book at GRIN:

http://www.grin.com/en/e-book/231538/a-survey-of-e-prescription-readiness-in-
selected-nigeria-hospitals

A SURVEY OF E-PRESCRIPTION READINESS IN SELECTED NIGERIA HOSPITALS

BY

KAZIR OLANREWAJU GANIU

TOSIN ADEWUNMI OGUNKOYODE

ADEBAYO OMOTOSHO

JULY 2013.

CERTIFICATION

We certify that Kazir Olanrewaju Ganiu, Tosin Adewunmi Ogunkoyode, of the Department of Computer Science and Technology, College of Information and Communication Technology, Bells university of Technology, Ota Ogun State, Nigeria carried out this study and to the best of our knowledge this work has been submitted for the award of a bachelor of technology degree in computer science.

....

....

PROF. D.O ADEWUNMI   SIGNATURE & DATE

(SUPERVISOR)

....

....

MR A. OMOTOSHO   SIGNATURE & DATE

(CO-SUPERVISOR)

....

....

MR. M.A. ADEGOKE   SIGNATURE & DATE

(HEAD OF DEPARMENT)

ii

DEDICATION

We dedicate this project to the entire staff of Bells university of Technology.

ACKNOWLEDGEMENTS

Firstly, We will want to thank our remarkable parents, Mr. and Mrs. Ganiu, Mr. and Mrs. Ogunkoyode without whom this period would not have been worthwhile.We also appreciate the effort made by our supervisors Prof. D.O Adewunmi and Mr A. Omotosho for taking out time to supervise this project; We also want to thank Mr M.A Adegoke and all staffs of College of Information and Communication Technology, could not have done this work without your help. Thank you.

We appreciate all members of staff of Lagos state university teaching hospital (LASUTH), University of Lagos teaching hospital (LUTH), Federal medical center (FMC Abeokuta) and The Neuropsychiatric hospital, Aro, Abeokuta who took out of their very precious time to answer the project questionnaire.

Lastly, Mr Adelabu Ayinla Ahmmed for taking out his precious time to help me go through this project.

TABLE OF CONTENTS

CHAPTER ONE

INTRODUCTION

CHAPTER TWO

LITERATURE REVIEW

CHAPTER THREE

METHODOLOGY

CHAPTER FOUR

ANALYSIS AND INTERPRETATION OF RESULT

CHAPTER FIVE

CONCLUSION AND RECOMMENDATION

LIST OF TABLES

LIST OF FIGURES

xi

ABSTRACT

This project is to survey electronic prescription readiness in Nigeria hospitals to know whether they are ready for electronic prescription or not. Electronic prescribing or e-prescribing, is computer-based electronic generation and transmission of a prescription. Prescribing systems helps to increase patient safety and increases prescribing accuracy, the system also helps to reduce costs through improved legibility. The motivation for e-prescribing is greater safety of drug use and the current unacceptable levels of adverse drug events. The aim of this study is to evaluate the readiness of Hospitals in Nigeria to adopt E-Prescription system for patient welfare and improved healthcare service delivery. With this research, problem of writing prescription for patients, which are prone to errors and sometimes result in patient harm, could be rectified if e-prescription is adopted.

A survey was conducted in Nigeria hospitals, which includes Lagos state university teaching hospital (LASUTH), University of Lagos teaching hospital (LUTH), Federal medical center (FMC Abeokuta) and The Neuropsychiatric hospital, Aro, Abeokuta. A well-structured questionnaire was also developed and was given out to doctors, pharmacists, pharmacy technicians and assistants present at the time of survey administration. Analysis of data was surveyed using MATLAB/Spss for analyzing of closed-ended questions; data was analyzed by using descriptive statistics, chi-square test and correlation co-efficient.

From the result of the analysis, it shows that EP system implementation is economically feasible on the side of an individual but on government side adequate funding for the achievement of EP system does not provide for the health sector to acquire the necessary resource and training skill.

CHAPTER ONE

INTRODUCTION

1.1 Background of the study

The major challenge of all health systems is to maximize the quality and the quantity of activities related to development or at least stabilization of health status of citizens, this maximization and optimization is often subject to budgetary and other constraints (EU, 2006).

Improvement in information and communication technology, being used in the Healthcare sector, are expected to be the solution for the reduction of rapidly increasing cost and the improvement of poor quality of healthcare services.

Medication prescribing is examined to be one of the most frequently used, powerful, therapeutic tools available to physicians. According to the definition provided by the e Health Initiative (EHI) electronic prescribing refers to "the use of computing devices to enter, modify, review and output or communicate drug prescriptions". (Perdikouri and Katharaki, 2011). Electronic prescribing has been proposed as an important strategy to reduce medication errors, improve the quality of patient care and create savings in healthcare costs (Tan et al, 2009) Electronic prescribing systems helps to increase patient safety and reduce costs through improved legibility since the misinterpretation of poorly handwritten prescriptions is the most frequently identified causes of medication errors. (Stranges et al, 2008). Despite the advantages of electronic prescribing the survey is to determine whether hospitals, pharmacists and physicians are ready for e-prescription, human factors could play a significant role in the success of the new technology and user satisfaction is one of them, from the view of physicians and pharmacists, changes to workflow, familiarization with the technology, and time commitment may overshadow the potential benefits of electronic prescribing. (Tan et al,2009) Therefore to ensure successful implementation of the system, implementers should frequently monitor areas of satisfaction and dissatisfaction among users, our survey is to determine the rate of how users are ready for e-prescription.

1.2 Statement of problem

Prescription of medications are among the most commonly used treatment in health care, but the process of managing written prescriptions and related telephone messages consumes substantial time for prescribers and their staff. Furthermore, these processes are prone to error and miscommunication, which sometimes result in patient harm. Electronic prescribing has been proposed as an important strategy to reduce medication errors, improve the quality of patient care and create savings in healthcare costs (Tan et al, 2009)

Many barriers have hindered the adoption of EHRs and e-prescribing systems, including the misalignment of financial incentives, the high cost of purchase, implementation and maintenance of systems; the immaturity of software products and vendors; the lack of integration between EHR systems;(Ash and Bates, 2005)and physician resistance.

A survey conducted by the Massachusetts Medical Society in 2003 revealed a large gap between physicians' perceived value of e prescribing and their intent to adopt this practice.(Ash and Bates, 2005)Their reluctance to embrace the changeover from paper to computerized systems was based, in large part, on the perception that e-prescribing is time-inefficient.

1.3 Motivation

E-prescribing systems have the potential to greatly reduce adverse pharmaceutical effects deriving from transcription, drug-drug interaction, allergies and dosage errors, to name a few. Indeed, studies show significant improvements associated with e-prescribing implementation, including an 86% decrease in serious medication errors and an increase in Medicare formulary adherence from 14% to 88%. (Speaker and Audet ,2006). Despite this evidence, however, providers have been slow to adopt e-prescribing technology due mainly to cost and regulatory constraints in the health industry.

According to the U.S. Department of Health and Human Services (HHS), while most industries spent $8,000 per worker for IT in the last decade, the health care industry invested only $1,000 per worker. (HR Policy Association, 2006). It should be noted that e-Prescription yields a variety of benefits of to patients, physicians and third parties (Petropoulou et al, 2011):

1.4 Aim

The aim of this study is to evaluate the readiness of Hospitals in Nigeria to adopt e-Prescription System for patient welfare and improved healthcare service delivery

1.5 Objectives

1. Carry out extensive literature review on related works on e-prescription adoption
2. To ascertain the acceptance level of e-prescription systems
3. To make recommendations based on findings

1.6 Methodology

This study was conducted in Nigeria hospitals; a survey questionnaire was developed after reviewing the literature and interviewing doctors and Pharmacists in the respective institutions. The survey questions addressed demographic information, experience in healthcare, experience with computers, and experience using an electronic prescription system. In addition to collecting information about the respondents, the survey also covers functionality, user training and support, and overall satisfaction.

Part of our preparation used to conduct the survey was a literature review and research. Academic journals, presentations, information materials, slides were also used to prepare for our study. Using these materials, we built a better understanding of the study. Majority of the materials we studied can be categorized in to some of the following: academic publications on assessment of electronic prescription systems, academic publications on satisfaction and adoption rate of electronic prescriptions systems. A cross-sectional survey was conducted at each hospital and a hardcopy self-administered anonymous questionnaire was given out to doctors, nurses, pharmacists and other medical practitioners. The completed form was collected by hand. Analysis of data was done using a computer programme called MATLAB was used. Data was analysed by using descriptive statistics, frequency distribution was drawn and also chi-square hypothesis test of Non-parametric is employed, to test for the significant of the three variables economic feasibility, technical feasibility and organizational feasibility of E-prescription system.

1.7 Significance of study

Problem of writing prescription for patients, which are prone to errors and sometimes result in patient harm, with this research the problem could be rectified if e-prescription is adopted. This research would also let us know if the physician, patients and pharmacist are ready for the e-prescription or not.

1.8 Scope

The survey was conducted in Nigeria hospitals, which include Lagos state university teaching hospital (LASUTH), University of Lagos teaching hospital (LUTH), Neuropsychiatric hospital, Aro, Abeokuta and Federal Medical Center Abeokuta.

CHAPTER TWO

LITERATURE REVIEW

2.1 Introduction

Paper prescriptions have been in use over the past year, written prescription became the sold means of communication between the physician and pharmacist. However they were drawbacks in this system, written prescription situation becomes even more complicated. The vision for electronic prescription systems was born in order to solve this problem and health informatics experts at the time thought that electronic prescription would be adopted in health industry within a few years, few dispute that e-prescription will improve the safety, quality and efficiency of patient care but low adoption rate persist. In this chapter, the review starts by defining e-prescription and describing its functionalities. Then the issues existing in paper prescription system. Next, review of related work from the perspectives of developed and developing countries.

2.2 E-Prescribing

Electronic prescribing has been proposed as an important strategy to reduce medication errors, improve the quality of patient care and create savings in healthcare costs (Woan et al, 2009).Electronic prescription systems allow the prescribing clinician to electronically send an accurate, error-free and understandable prescription directly to the pharmacy. E-Prescribing is the use of healthcare technology to improve prescription accuracy, increase patient safety and reduce costs, as well as enable secure, bi-directional, electronic connectivity between physician practices and pharmacies. This is achieved by providing prescribers a secure means of electronically accessing up-to-date health plan formulary, patient eligibility and medication history at the point of care and securely transmitting the prescription electronically into the pharmacy's computer system. (Rxhub, 2008).

2.2.1. E-prescription and paper prescription system

With the definition of e-prescription defined earlier, essential differences between e-prescription system and paper system which is also known as the traditional system, patients visit their health care provider for medical consultation, and after assessment of the medical condition of the patient the doctor writes off a prescription on a paper. The prescription is then signed and given to the patient, then the patient authorized representative presents the prescription to a pharmacy of his/her choice for getting the prescribed medicines while the electronic prescription which is the transmission and processing of medical information contained within medicinal prescriptions through all components of the prescription system, from the initial prescribing of the drugs, through dispensation to the patient, to the eventual close of transaction at some prescription-processing agent.

Table 2.1 Difference between paper prescription and e-prescription

Paper system	e-prescription system
High rate of prescription fraud	Low rate of prescription fraud
High rate of prescription error	Low rate of error prescription
Due to error, it increase cost	It saves cost
Highly susceptible to adverse drug effect	Low adverse drug effect

2.2.2 Issues of paper prescription

Today most medical prescriptions are typically handwritten or printed on paper and hand-delivered to pharmacists. Paper-based medical prescription has generated and still generating major concerns as the incidences of prescription errors have been increasing and causing problems to patients, including deaths. Though paper prescription system has been in existence

6

for years, it is easily influenced for different types of errors at each step in the process. These errors are the result of difficulties such as

I.   Lack of medical information integrity and sharing

II. Drug cross-reactivity and complications

III. Incorrect or inadequate physicians knowledge about the new medications

IV. Slow prescription ordering and dispensing process

V.   Security and privacy issues

VI. Lack of standardization of technologies and protocols used

VII. Administrative and organizational issues such as pharmaceutical benefits and billing process.

Fatal health problems can arise due to bad and illegible written prescriptions, errors in dosage and unanticipated drug interactions, communication errors committed during ordering, dispensing and administering of drugs, and dosing mistakes such as incorrect dose of drug and incorrect frequency of drug intake, and lack of reliable health information. Most of these errors of paper prescription system could be reduced by electronic prescription. Though e-prescription is simple and straightforward, it has not yet been widely adopted.

2.2.3 Types of an e-Prescribing system

There are two choices of an e-prescribing system; it is either a stand- alone system, or e-prescribing within an EHR system. There are pros and cons of each option in terms of cost, level of effort and time to select and deploy, impact on practice workflow and productivity initially and over time, and interoperability with other electronic health information systems.

2.2.3.1 A stand-alone system is less costly and less difficult to implement, and thus can be implemented faster than an EHR system. This may be an important consideration for practices that wish to be eligible for Medicare's e-prescribing bonus that begins on January 1, 2009. E-prescribing systems store and manage patient data specific to the prescribing process (e.g., medication history, medication allergies, etc.). E-prescribing software is offered in two forms: (a) a software package you acquire and download to your office computer system, or more commonly; (b) through the Internet, connecting with an e-prescribing software application service provider (ASP), to whom you pay usage fees.

In terms of e-prescribing hardware, physician practices have many choices including: hand- held devices, tablet personal computers, desktop personal computers, and other hardware made available by technology vendors.

Many believe that a stand-alone e-prescribing system can serve as a pathway to an EHR system, allowing prescribers to become more technologically proficient and comfortable with using electronic systems to support and improve patient care. When implementing a stand-alone system, it is important to plan how you will eventually transition to an EHR system.

2.2.3.2 An EHR system with an integrated e-prescribing module it gives the advantage of having immediate electronic access to all patient data stored in the EHR system, including diagnoses, problem lists, clinical notes, laboratory and radiology results and orders, adding to a clinician's ability to make the most informed medication choices for their patients. EHR systems may also often offer an extensive range of clinical decision support, including notification of needed screening tests, immunizations, etc.

Physician practices are increasingly using e-prescribing within an EHR system, due to the EHR system's more comprehensive functionality, which enables greater gains in quality and safety. Currently, more than 50 EHR systems offer integrated e-prescribing. For practices that are committed to full automation and interoperability with other providers and sources of patient information, an EHR system with e-prescribing would be the better choice.

EHR systems are significantly more costly and difficult to implement than stand-alone e-prescribing applications. (e-health initiative, 2008)

2.2.4 Standards for e-prescribing systems

Physicians, pharmacy dispensers, software vendors, insurers, and patients must work together so that an integrated e-prescribing become a reality. To be able to share critical information across various health care settings, systems must be able to interoperate with one another. The inability for multiple systems to share information with a standard format and vocabulary has been a hurdle to effective implementation of e-prescribing (Perdikouri and Kathraki , 2011). The principal standards proposed for use by e- prescribing systems include:

  I. Medication History standard: intended to provide a uniform means for prescribers, dispensers, and payers to communicate about the list of drugs that have been dispensed to a patient

II. Formulary and Benefits standard: intended to provide prescribers with information about a patient's drug coverage at the point of care. (Information may include whether drugs are considered to be "on formulary," alternative medications for those drugs not on formulary, rules for prior authorization and step therapy, and the cost to the patient for one drug option versus another

III. Prescription Fill Status Notification standard : serving the purpose of notifying the prescriber about whether a patient has picked up a prescribed medication at the pharmacy, so that compliance or not compliance of patient could be estimated

IV. Prior Authorization standard :which refers to the process by which insurers require patients to receive approval before certain drugs will be covered

V. Structured and Codified SIG standard: describes patient instructions for taking medications, called the signature, commonly abbreviated SIG. (The fact that for the present, there is no standardized format or vocabulary for SIGs, leaves room for misinterpretation and error, jeopardizing patient safety

VI. Rx Norm standard: is expected to face the problem of the existence of currently multiple databases of drug names, forms, and dosages.

2.3 Benefit of e-prescription

It should be noted that e-prescribing yields a variety of benefits of to patients, physicians and third parties such as (Petropoulou et al, 2005):

I. Patients: convenience (prescriptions and medications ready for pick-up), fewer difficulties over prescription insurance coverage (therapy starts without delay), satisfaction (simplification of procedure, especially of the one related to renewals of prescriptions), safety (legible prescriptions that have been checked for harmful interactions).

II. Pharmacists: fewer mistakes because of misread, more time spent to critical issues concerning drug therapy matters, competitive advantage over pharmacists who do not adopt e-prescribing, simplification of the claiming procedure.

III. Physicians: on line access to patient's information, better formulary adherence and alignment with guidelines, on line notification of drug interactions and review of the cost of prescription produced.

9

IV. Health Authorities: less paperwork, less unproductive time spent on bureaucratic procedures, reduced medication cost by supporting the prescribing of generic, information on the prescribing habits of doctors and health status of citizens.

2.4 How e-Prescribing works

Creating and managing prescriptions electronically involves several steps, as illustrated in the process map below.

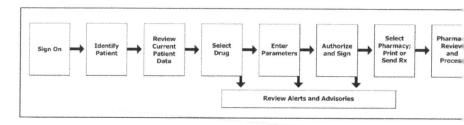

Figure 2.1 Stages for Creating and Managing a Prescription Electronically(e-health initiative, 2008)

A physician signs in by performing some authentication to prove his or her identity.

The physician identifies the patient record within the e-prescribing system.

Typing demographic information to the e-prescribing system can identify patient records.

The physicians also review the medical history, entering and editing a prescription.

The physicians then authorize and sign the prescribed medications, select the pharmacy; print or send the medications prescribed.

Finally the pharmacy review and process the drugs prescribed.

2.5 Limitations to e-Prescribing adoption

E-prescribing can smooth run work processes and make the system run efficiently if the right tools are available in the right setting. Change can be difficult; e-prescribing may enable your practice to more effectively manage medications for your patients. (e-health initiative 2008) Challenges that have restricted more global adoption are described below.

10

I. **Financial Cost and Return on Investment (ROI):** Prescribers, especially those in small practices and in inner city or rural settings, may believe they bear more than their fair share of the cost of e-prescribing, since other stakeholders also benefit from the savings and quality improvements that are achieved, or receive fees from the use of e-prescribing. Physician practices need to invest in hardware and software, and cost estimates vary depending on whether an EHR system is adopted or a stand-alone e-prescribing system is used.

II. **Change Management:** It is important not to undervalue the change management challenges associated with transitioning from paper prescribing to e-prescribing. In a busy practice setting where providers and their staff are accustomed to their current management of patient prescriptions, change management is important. If some of the providers and staff are particularly technology averse, it can be difficult to get everyone onboard with such a dramatic change.

III. **Workflow:** New systems, particularly in the beginning, are likely to add time to tasks like creating new prescriptions or capturing preferred pharmacy information at patient intake, and this can be a barrier. Workflow changes are greater with a full EHR system as compared to stand-alone e-prescribing systems, but either way, practices often experience lost productivity during the transition while they modify the practice workflow and become adept at using the system.

IV. **Limitations on E-Prescribing System Remote Access:** There are often no easy remote access options. In rural areas there may not be many options for consistent remote access services due to cell phone gaps for digital service and limitations of broadband Internet service.

V. **Patient Acceptance/Usage Issues:** Some patients may not feel comfortable with electronic prescriptions and demand their clinician provide a paper prescription. Also, patients who travel frequently, or are otherwise away from home for extended periods may feel more comfortable having a written prescription to take with them.

VI. **Medication History and Medication Reconciliation:** E-prescribing can help provide information to prescribers at the point of care on what medications their patients are taking, and have taken in the past. However, it is difficult to place absolute confidence in the completeness and currency of this information, since medication histories must be reconciled from multiple sources. Prescribers should always consult with their patients about what medications they are taking to validate the medication history information that is available through e-prescribing and update the records accordingly.

VII. **Hardware and Software Selection:** Choosing the right software and hardware and supporting it after installation can be a daunting task for some physician practices, especially small practices that are extremely busy, experiencing declining reimbursements, and lack expert information technology staff. Some struggle with how to get started, vendor selection, negotiation, implementation and long term support.

2.6 Tele-pharmacy

It is the innovative approaches in providing pharmacy services during a time of pharmacist shortage or 24 hours base time. Tele-pharmacy involves integrating telecommunications, information system pharmacy software, and remote controlled dispensing technology to support a pharmacy model in which a central pharmacy is electronically linked to single or multiple physician offices, local and remote clinics, emergency rooms, health and surgical centers, long term care facilities, correctional and rehabilitative facilities or other difficult to serve points of outpatient health care.

Tele-pharmacy means electronic transmission of a prescription order from the remote location to the central pharmacy. There, the order is reviewed and verified by the pharmacist who then authorizes and oversees automated dispensing of the needed medication from the pre-filled drug cabinet at a distance. If necessary, web camera or real time videoconference can enable face-to-face consultation between the pharmacist, the physician and the patient. Tele-pharmacy offers numerous advantages for the patient, including increased convenience, reduced waiting time, and increased access to medications and experts in locations where a full-time pharmacist may not be available. The development of a Tele-pharmacy-enabled model of pharmacy practices is imperative for the pharmacists. (Petropoulou et al, 2005).

2.7 Review of related work

Tan et al, 2009, investigated the satisfaction level of prescription systems implemented in Singapore by surveying about 9 national health care groups. The overall level of satisfaction with electronic prescribing was high. Doctors and pharmacists reported a high degree of agreement that electronic prescribing reduces prescribing errors and interventions, and they did not want to go back to the paper-based system. Only 56.9% of the pharmacy respondents expressed satisfaction with the review function of the electronic prescription system and only 51.8% and 60% were satisfied when processing prescriptions that included items to be purchased from an external pharmacy or prescriptions with amendments. The results also revealed that satisfaction with the system was more associated with users' perceptions about the electronic prescription system's impact on productivity than quality of care.

In Perdikouri and Katharaki, (2011) the authors reviewed what should be considered when implementing and evaluating an e-prescribing system and they used Greece as case study, and secondly to combine the relevant findings with the current situation in Greece in order to the key factors that will determine the acceptance and the success of such an attempt The analysis reveals that standards, appropriate coding and interoperability are of great interest and can assure the long-term viability of e- prescribing systems, while the participation of all stakeholders (clinicians, patients, healthcare providers and healthcare organizations) is considered to be indispensable for the success of both implementation and function of these systems. However the general principles should be modified in order to fit the special socioeconomic needs that e prescribing is expected to fulfill.

In Went et al (2008) the authors investigated if an electronic prescribing system designed specifically to reduce errors would lead to fewer errors in prescribing medicines in a secondary care setting. The electronic system was compared with paper prescription charts on 16 intensive care patients to assess any change in the number of prescribing errors. The overall level of compliance with nationally accepted standards was significantly higher with the electronic system (91.67%) compared to the paper system (46.73%). Electronically generated prescriptions were found to contain significantly fewer deviations (28 in 329 prescriptions, 8.5%) than the written prescriptions (208 in 408 prescriptions, 51%).

The results conclude that the reduction in prescribing errors with the electronic system is significant. This study confirms the importance of involving clinicians in the design and development of an electronic system to produce a solution that is not only accepted and easily adopted by users but which also reduces the numbers of errors made.

In Ardava et al (2010) the authors performed a research to clarify the attitude of individual pharmacies towards electronic Prescription and necessary amount of investment for introduction and maintenance for this innovation using Latvian pharmacies as case study. The research is based on the attitude of the owners of the pharmacies towards introduction of electronic prescription that is to be sized up through providing a questioning to them. The finds produced research has been displayed that the owners of the pharmacies have been currently showing a vague notion about efficiency of the introduction of the electronic prescription. Problems would be risen if individual pharmacies will have to be financing the introduction of pharmacies information systems by themselves. After study of the problem, there would be several solutions: joint venture of pharmacies, government support, attraction of EU structural funds etc.

In Bell et all (2004) the authors aimed to develop a conceptual work for predict the effects of another designs for outpatient e-prescribing systems. Based on literature review and on telephone interviews with e-prescribing vendors, the authors identified well defined e-prescribing functional capabilities and developed a conceptual framework for evaluating e-prescribing systems' potential effects based on their potentials. The proposed framework for evaluating e-prescribing systems is organized using a process model of medication management. Evidence was identified to support specific effects for the functional potentials. The evidence also shows that a functional capability with generally positive effects which also could be applied in a way that creates unintended hazards. It was concluded that the proposed conceptual framework supports the integration of available evidence in considering the full range of effects from e-prescribing design alternatives. More research is needed into the effects of specific e-prescribing functional alternatives. Until more is known, e-prescribing initiatives should include provisions to monitor for unintended hazards.

In Tamblyn et al (2006) the authors developed and evaluated the acceptability and use of an integrated electronic prescribing and drug management system (MOXXI) for primary care physicians. MOXXI was developed to enhance patient safety by integrating patient demographics, retrieving active drugs from pharmacy systems, generating an automated problem list, acceptability, and use was conducted using audit trails, questionnaires, standardized tasks, and information from comprehensive health insurance databases. Physician speed in using MOXXI has done well substantially in the first three months; however, Physicians wrote electronic prescriptions in 36.9 per 100 visits and reviewed the patient's drug profile in 12.6 per 100 visits. Physicians rated printed prescriptions, the current drug list, and the re-prescribing function as one of the most beneficial aspects of the system. they ended up concluding that the Primary care physicians believed an integrated electronic prescribing and drug management system would improve continuity of care, and they were more likely to use the system for patients with more complex, fragmented care.

Shams, (2011), also presented a survey result of overall satisfaction which integrated e-prescription was high. Physicians, pharmacy staff and nurses highly agreed that the EPS reduced prescribing errors and they did not want to go back to the paper based prescription system. Pharmacy staff and nurses viewed the EPS more positively and were more satisfied with it than were physicians. It was also found that 74% of patients who responded to the survey were either satisfied or very satisfied with the EPS and preferred it over paper-based prescriptions. In conclusion, the majority of stakeholders were generally satisfied with the current status of the EPS, but they also perceived a few key weaknesses. A total of 12 recommendations were offered to improve the e-prescription in clinical settings in the Sultanate of Oman.

15

2.8 Concluding remarks

After an extensive review of different development and evaluation of e-prescription , it confirm the importance of e-prescription but however publications studied also refused to thoroughly note some of the challenges the electronic prescription faced before adoption, and also government impact on electronic prescription systems.

CHAPTER THREE

METHODOLOGY

3.1 Introduction

Survey of e-prescription has been extensively reviewed in different development and evaluation of e-prescription , it confirm the importance of e-prescription but however publications studied also refuse to note some of the challenges the electronic prescription faced before adoption, and also government impact on electronic prescription systems. More research is needed into the effects of specific e-prescribing functional alternatives. Until more is known, e-prescribing initiatives should include provisions to monitor for unintended hazards, this chapter contains the methods in which how survey will be developed, survey implementation and the proposed statistical model for analyzing the result. The objective of this research is to access the readiness of electronic prescribing implementation in Nigeria.

3.2 Survey development

The survey questionnaire was developed after reviewing the several publications. Survey questions addressed demographic information, experience in healthcare, and experience using the electronic prescription system. The questionnaire consists of three sections and twenty questions. The sections include economic feasibility, technical feasibility and organization feasibility section. The economic feasibility of the survey contain seven questions and to determine the economic benefits to the hospitals that the proposed system will provide, also structure to elicit user satisfaction with a variety of electronic prescription functions based on the list of tasks carried out by the doctors, pharmacists and nurses in the workflow and will also structure to draw out user satisfaction with the ease of working paperless, the technical feasibility contains seven questions which is focused on gaining an understanding of the present technical resources of hospitals and their applicability to the expected needs of the system, the organizational feasibility contain six questions the section is structure to determine whether the current new system will fit into the organisation and meet the new system goals and objectives, it also to determine whether the new system will have enough support from users to be successfully adopted and whether users can operate the system. The respondent are to respond or give answers to this survey template by ticking from a range of five values from "Strongly disagree" to strongly agree (i.e. strongly disagree, disagree, Not sure, Agree, Strongly agree). The survey also asked respondents to indicate their agreement or disagreement with statements regarding the adequacy of training and ongoing support as well as their perception regarding the impact of the use of electronic prescription on prescription errors and interventions. The response categories for these questions include strongly agree, agree, not sure, disagree and strongly disagree.

3.3 Survey implementation

The survey was conducted in Nigeria hospitals, which include Lagos state university teaching hospital (LASUTH), University of Lagos teaching hospital (LUTH) , The Neuropsychiatric hospital, Aro, Abeokuta and Federal Medical Center Abeokuta.The following hospitals were chosen because they are federal and state standard hospitals in south west of Nigeria and project team location. Hardcopy self-administered anonymous questionnaires were given out to doctors, pharmacists, pharmacy technicians and assistants present at the time of survey administration. The completed questionnaires were collected by hand.

3.4Data collection instrument

A questionnaire was chosen as data collection instrument. A questionnaire is a printed self-report form designed to elicit information that can be obtained through the written responses of the subjects. A questionnaire was design that categories into two sections respondents characteristics, and question pertain to the subject.

3.5 Matlab overview

MATLAB is a high-level language and interactive environment for numerical computation, visualization, and programming. Using MATLAB, you can analyse data, develop algorithms, and create models and applications. The language, tools, and built-in math functions enable you to explore multiple approaches and reach a solution faster than with spreadsheets or traditional programming languages, such as C/C++ or Java. You can use MATLAB for a range of applications, including signal processing and communications, image and video processing, control systems, test and measurement, computational finance, and computational biology. More than a million engineers and scientists in industry and academia use MATLAB, the language of technical computing.

3.6 The matlab language

The matlab language provides native support for the vector and matrix operations that are fundamental to solving engineering and scientific problems, enabling fast development and execution.

With the matlab language, someone can write programs and develop algorithms faster than with traditional languages because you do not need to perform low- level administrative tasks such as declaring variables, specifying data types, and allocating memory. In many cases, the support for vector and matrix operations eliminates the need for for-loops. As a result, one line of Matlab code can often replace several lines of C or C++ code.

Matlab provides features of traditional programming languages, including flow control, error handling, and object-oriented programming (OOP).Someone can use fundamental data types or advanced data structures, or you can define custom data types.

Someone can also produce immediate results by interactively executing commands one at a time. This approach can let you quickly explore multiple options and iterate to an optimal solution. You can also capture the interactive steps as scripts and functions to reuse and automate your work.

Matlab add-on products provide built- in algorithms for signal processing and communications, image and video processing, control systems, and many other domains. By combining these algorithms with your own, you can build complex programs and applications.

3.7Data analysis

After the data was collected it was organised and analysed. For analysing of closed-ended questions, a computer programme called MATLAB/Spss was used. Data was analysed by using descriptive statistics, frequency distribution was drawn and also chi-square hypothesis test of Non-parametric is employed. To test for the significant of the three variables economic feasibility, technical feasibility and organizational feasibility of e-prescription system.

RESEARCH QUESTIONNAIRE

Dear Respondent,

This questionnaire is designed to acquire relevant information for the successful completion of a project titled " SURVEY OF E – PRESCRIPTION READINESS IN NIGERIA ", please tick your response. Your honest response will be highly appreciated even as you are assured of the confidentiality of your response.

Thanks.

Please tick the box below to answer the following question

Sex: Male   □Female□

Profession:

Region:

Age:

Years in practices:

Name of hospital:

Economic feasibility	Strongly Agree	Agree	Not sure	Disagree	Strongly disagree
Do you think the hospital firm can afford to improve the internet network?					
Do you think paper prescriptions are prone to errors?					
Do you think the hospital firm can afford to get all physicians computer?					
Do you think you waste much calling card and time calling the pharmacy for corrections?					
Do you think paper prescription is effective in your job?					
Do you think using e-prescription system will improve the quality of health service?					
Do you think e-prescription system will save your time and reduce error?					

Technical feasibility	Strongly Agree	Agree	Not sure	Disagree	Strongly disagree
Do you think using computer for electronic prescription would make your work more effective and accurate?					
Do you think the internet network in the hospital is good?					
Do you think you are good at operating computer system?					
Do you think you are fast in responding to training on new device?					
Do you think the e-prescription system would be easy to use?					
Do you think you are really motivated to pick up the new electronic prescription system?					
Do you think you have ability to use the electronic prescription system?					

Organizational feasibility	Strongly agree	Agree	Not sure	Disagree	Strongly disagree
Does the government respond well to the need of the hospital?					
Would learning to operate the computer be easy for you?					
Do you think it will be easy to adapt to the new workflow?					
Can the hospital firm manage and be consistent the system over a long time?					
Do you think the your hospital firm would be ready to adopt the new system based on the infrastructural facilities?					
Do you think the patient will be ready to adopt the new system?					

21

CHAPTER FOUR

ANALYSIS AND INTERPRETATION OF RESULT

4.1 Introduction

This chapter shows the result of analysis performed, and also showing the respective tables for Data analyzed by using descriptive statistics, frequency distribution was drawn and also chi-square hypothesis test of Non-parametric was employed. Data was obtained from four hospitals which include Lagos university teaching hospital (LUTH), Lagos state university teaching hospital(LASUTH), The Neuropsychiatric hospital, Aro Abeokuta, Federal medical centre, idiaba Abeokuta (FMC).

4.2 Frequency distribution table of demographic

Table 4.1 Frequency distribution table of gender

Sex	Frequency	Percentage of gender
Male	29	69.0476
Female	13	30.9523

Table 4.1 represent a Frequency distribution table of gender that shows the gender frequency distribution of the respondent's of male and female in which the frequency of male is 29and percentage is 69.05% and the frequency of female is 13 and percentage 30.95% out of 42 respondents administered from questionnaire.

Table 4.2 Frequency distribution table of profession

Profession	Frequency	Percentage of profession
Doctor	21	50.0000
Pharmacist	12	28.5714
Nurse	5	11.9048
Medical	4	9.5238

22

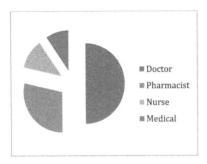

Figure 4.1 Frequency distribution pie chart of profession

Table 4.2 and Fig. 4.1 represents a frequency distribution table and pie chart of profession that shows the frequency distribution of respondents in relating to their professions, in which the doctors frequency is 21 out of 42with percentage of 50.00% and pharmacist in which the frequency is 12 out of 42 with the percentage of 28.57%,the Nurses percentage is 5 out of 42and percentage 11.90% and Medical Practitioner frequency is 4 out of 42 with percentage of 9.52

Table 4.3 Frequency distribution table of age

Age	Frequency	Percentage of age
0-30	15	35.71
30-40	21	50
40-60	6	14.29

Table 4.3 represent a frequency distribution table of age that shows the frequency distribution of respondent's age wise with the range of 0 to 30 years and frequency 15 and the percentage 35.71%, range of 30 to 40 years with the frequency of twenty-one and percentage 50%, and lastly the age range of 40 to 60 years with the frequency of six and percentage of 14.29%.

Table 4.4 frequency distribution table of year in practice

Years in practice	Frequency	Percentage of years in practice
0-5	16	38.1
10-15	18	42.86
15-20	6	14.29

Table 4.4 represent frequency distribution table of year in practice that shows the frequency distribution of the respondent's that administered the questionnaire in relating to their year of practice their profession with the range of zero to five years and frequency sixteen and the percentage 38.1%, range of ten to fifteen years with the frequency of eighteen and percentage 42.86%, and lastly the year in practice range of fifteen to twenty years with the frequency of six and percentage of 14.29%.

Economic feasibility

H_0 : The economical feasibility of E-prescription usage is significant.

Table 4.5 Test statistic table for Economic feasibility

Test Statistics

	Economic feasibility
Chi-Square	18.405a
Df	9
Approx. Sig	.031

Table 4.5 is test-statistic table that shows the chi-square statistical test of the H_0 (null hypothesis) as a one-sample test. From the table it appears that the null hypothesis rejected and accepted the

alternative hypothesis because (0.031 < 5% level of significant). This implies that economic feasibility of E-prescription usage is significant.

Table 4.6 Frequency distribution table of respondent on internet network improvement

Internet network	Frequency	Percentage of ability to improve internet network
Missing	1	2.3810
Not Sure	2	4.7619
Agree	21	50.0000
Strongly Agree	18	42.8571

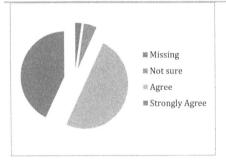

Figure 4.2 Frequency distribution pie chart of respondent on internet network improvement

Table 4.6 and Fig. 4.2 represents a frequency distribution table and pie chart of frequency distribution of respondent on the ability of the hospital firm to improve the internet network that shows the frequency distribution of respondents in relating to internet network improvement on whether the hospital firm can improve on the internet network; in which out of 42 questionnaires distributed frequency of 1 and percentage 2.38% was left unfilled which represent Missing, respondents that are Not Sure with frequency of 2 and percentage of 4.76%, respondents that Agreed and Strongly Agree with the frequencies of 21 and 18 and percentages of 50% and 42.86 % respectively.

Table 4.7 Frequency distribution table of respondent on if e-prescription will improve quality of service

EP improve quality of service	Frequency	Percentage of EP improve quality of service
Missing	1	2.3810
Not Sure	3	7.429
Agree	12	28.5714
Strongly Agree	26	61.9048

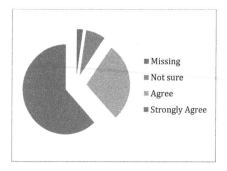

Figure 4.3 Frequency distribution pie chart of respondent on if e-prescription will improve quality of service.

Table 4.7 and Fig. 4.3 represents a frequency distribution table and pie chart of frequency distribution of respondent that shows the frequency distribution of the respondents on how e-prescription will improve quality of service in relating on if e-prescription will improve quality of service; in which out of 42 questionnaires distributed frequency of 1 and percentage 2.38% was

left unfilled which represent Missing, respondents that are Not Sure with frequency of 3 and percentage of 7.14%, respondents that Agreed and Strongly Agree that e-prescription will improve quality of service are frequencies of 12 and 26 and percentages of 28.57% and 61.90% respectively.

26

Table 4.8 Frequency distribution table of respondent on if e-prescription saves time

E-prescription save time	Frequency	Percentage of EP save time
Missing	1	2.3810
Disagree	1	2.3810
Not Sure	5	11.9048
Agree	15	35.7143
Strongly Agree	20	47.6190

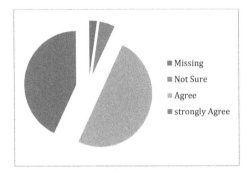

■ Missing
■ Not Sure
▩ Agree
■ strongly Agree

Figure 4.4 Frequency distribution table of respondent on if e-prescription saves time

Table 4.8 and Fig. 4.4 represents a frequency distribution table and pie chart that shows the frequency distribution of the respondents in relating to how e-prescription will save time; in which out of 42 questionnaires distributed frequency of 1 and percentage 2.38% was left unfilled which represent Missing, respondents that Disagree and are Not Sure are frequencies of 1and 5 and percentages of 2.38% and 11.90%, respondents that Agreed and Strongly Agree that e-prescription will save time are the frequencies of 15 and 20 and percentages of 35.71% and 47.61 % respectively.

Table 4.9 Frequency distribution table of respondent on hospital affordability of computers to physicians

Hospital affordability of computers to physicians	Frequency	Percentage of hospital affordability of computers
Missing	1	2.3810
Not Sure	2	4.7619
Agree	21	50.0000
Strongly Agree	18	42.8571

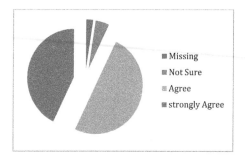

Figure 4.5 Frequency distribution pie chart of respondent on hospital affordability of computers to physicians

Table 4.9 and Fig. 4.5 represents a frequency distribution table and pie chart that shows the frequency distribution of the respondent's in relating to hospital affordability of computers to physicians, in which out of 42 questionnaires distributed frequency of 1 and percentage 2.38% was left unfilled which represent Missing, respondents that are Not Sure with frequency of 2 and percentage of 4.76%, respondents that Agreed and Strongly Agree with the frequencies of 21 and 18 and percentages of 50% and 42.86 % respectively with 2.38% Missing, 4.76% Not Sure, 50.00% Agree and 42.86% Strongly Agree.

28

Technical feasibility

H_0 :The technical feasibility of E-prescription usage is significant

Table 4.10 Test statistic table of technical feasibility

Test Statistics

Test Statistics	Technical Feasibility
Chi-Square	12.000a
df	12
Approx. Sig.	.446

Table 4.10 shows the chi-square statistical test of the H_0 (null hypothesis) as a one-sample test. From the table it appears that the null hypothesis accepted; because (0.446>5% level of significant). This implies that technical feasibility of E-prescription usage is insignificant.

Table 4.11 Frequency distribution table of respondent on Internet network qualities

Internet network	Frequency	Percentage of internet network qualities
Missing	1	2.3810
Strongly Disagree	2	4.7619
Disagree	16	38.0952
Not sure	1	2.3810
Agree	7	16.6667
Strongly Agree	15	35.7143

29

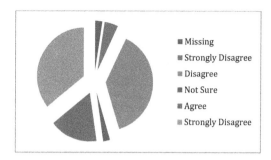

- Missing
- Strongly Disagree
- Disagree
- Not Sure
- Agree
- Strongly Disagree

Figure 4.6 Frequency distribution pie chart of respondent on Internet network qualities

Table 4.11 and Fig. 4.6 represents a frequency distribution table and pie chart that shows the frequency distribution of the respondents in relating to how good the internet network of the hospital firm, in which out of 42 questionnaires distributed frequency of 1 and percentage 2.38% was left unfilled which represent Missing, respondents that Strongly Disagree with the frequency of 2 and percentage of 4.76%, and respondents that Disagree and are Not Sure are frequencies of 16 and 1 and percentages of 38.09% and 2.38%, respondents that Agreed and Strongly Agree are frequencies of 7 and 15 and percentages of 16.67% and 35.71 % respectively.

Table 4.12 Frequency distribution table of respondent on Ability to operate computer

Ability to operate computer	Frequency	Percentage of respondent on Ability to operate computer
Missing	2	4.7619
Disagree	2	4.7619
Not Sure	2	4.7619
Agree	20	47.619
Strongly Agree	16	38.0952

Table 4.12 represent a Frequency distribution table of respondent on ability to operate computer that shows the frequency distribution of the respondents in relating to how good they are in operating computer (technical), in which out of 42 questionnaires distributed frequency of 2 and percentage 4.76% was left unfilled which represent Missing, respondents that Disagree and are

30

Not Sure with frequencies of 2 and percentages of 4.76% each, respondents that Agreed and Strongly Agree with the frequencies of 20 and 16 and percentages of 47.62% and 38.10 % respectively.

Table 4.13 Frequency distribution table of respondent on response to training

Response to training	Frequency	Percentage of response to training
Missing	1	2.3810
'Not Sure	2	4.7619
Agree	19	45.2381
'Strongly Agree	20	47.6190

Table 4.13 represent frequency distribution table of respondent on response to training that shows the frequency distribution of the respondent's in relating to response to training (technical) on good they are at learning new technology, in which out of 42 questionnaires distributed frequency of 1 and percentage 2.38% was left unfilled which represent Missing, respondents that are Not Sure with frequency of 2 and percentage of 4.76%, respondents that Agreed and Strongly Agree with the frequencies of 19 and 20 and percentages of 45.24% and 47.62% respectively.

Table 4.14 Frequency distribution table of respondent on e-prescription ease of use

E-prescription ease your work	Frequency	Percentage of EP ease to your work
Missing	1	2.3810
Disagree	1	2.3810
Not Sure	13	30.9524
Agree	20	47.6190
Strongly Agree	7	16.6667

31

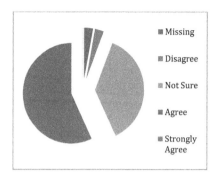

Figure 4.7 Frequency distribution pie chart of respondent on e-prescription ease of use

Table 4.14 and Fig. 4.7 represents a frequency distribution table and pie chart that shows the frequency distribution of the respondent's in relating on how E-prescription makes your work easier, in which out of 42 questionnaires distributed frequency of 1 and percentage 2.38% was left unfilled which represent Missing, respondents that Disagree and are Not Sure with frequencies of 1 and 13 and percentage of 2.38% and 30.95% respectively, respondents that Agreed and Strongly Agree with the frequencies of 20 and 7 and percentages of 47.62% and 16.67 % respectively.

Table 4.15 Frequency distribution table of respondent on ability to use computer

Ability to use computer	Frequency	Percentage of ability to use computer
'Strongly Disagree	1	2.3810
Not Sure	3	7.1429
Agree	22	52.3810
Strongly Agree	16	38.0952

Table 4.15 represent a frequency distribution table of respondent on ability to use computer that shows the frequency distribution of the respondents in relating to Ability to use computer (technical);in which out of 42 questionnaires distributed , respondents that Strongly Disagree and are Not Sure with frequencies of 1 and 3 and percentage of 2.38% and 7.14%, respondents that

32

Agreed and Strongly Agree with the frequencies of 22 and 16 and percentages of 52.38% and 38.09 % respectively.

Organizational feasibility

H_0 : The organizational feasibility of E-prescription usage is significant

Table 4.16 Test statistic table of Organizational feasibility

Test Statistic

	Organizational Feasibility
Chi-Square	15.359a
Df	7
Approx. Sig.	.032

Table 4.16 represent a test-statistics table that shows the chi-square statistical test of the H_0 (null hypothesis) as a one-sample test. From the table it appears that the null hypothesis rejected and accepted the alternative hypothesis because (0.032 < 5% level of significant). This implies that organizational feasibility of E-prescription usage is significant.

Table 4.17 Frequency distribution table of respondent on government response to hospital needs

Government response to hospital needs	Frequency	Percentage of government response to hospital need
Missing	1	2.3810
Strongly Disagree	5	11.9028
Disagree	17	40.4762
Not Sure	15	35.7143
Agree	3	7.1429
Strongly Agree	1	2.3810

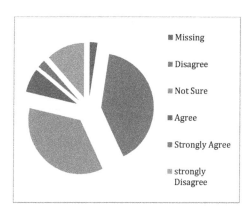

Figure 4.8 Frequency distribution pie chart of respondent on government response to hospital needs

Table 4.17 and Fig. 4.8 represents a frequency distribution table and pie chart that shows the frequency distribution of the respondents in relating to how government respond to the hospital needs (organizational), in which out of 42 questionnaires distributed frequency of 1 and percentage 2.38% was left unfilled which represent Missing, respondents that Strongly Disagree with the frequency of 5 and percentage of 11.90%, and respondents that Disagree and are Not Sure are frequencies of 17 and 15 and percentages of 40.48% and 35.71%, respondents that Agreed and Strongly Agree are frequencies of 3 and 1 and percentages of 7.14% and 2.38% respectively.

34

Table 4.18 Frequency distribution table of respondent on how long hospital can manage e-prescription

Hospital manage	Frequency	Percentage of hospital management of e-prescription
Missing	1	2.3810
Disagree	1	2.3810
Not Sure	26	61.9048
Agree	10	23.8095
Strongly Agree	4	9.5238

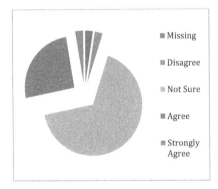

Figure 4.9 Frequency distribution pie chart of respondent on how long hospital can manage e-prescription

Table 4.18 and Fig. 4.9 represents a frequency distribution table and pie chart that shows the frequency distribution of the respondents in relating to how long the hospital can manage electronic prescription, in which out of 42 questionnaires distributed frequency of 1 and percentage 2.38% was left unfilled which represent Missing, respondents that Disagree and are Not Sure with frequencies of 1 and 26 and percentage of 2.38% and 61.90%, respondents that Agreed and Strongly Agree with the frequencies of 10 and 4 and percentages of 23.81% and 9.52 % respectively.

Table 4.19 Frequency distribution table of respondent on hospital readiness to adopt e-prescription

Hospital readiness to adopt	Frequency	Percentage of hospital readiness to adopt
Missing	1	2.3810
Disagree	1	2.3810
Not Sure	17	40.4762
Agree	18	42.8571
Strongly Agree	5	11.9048

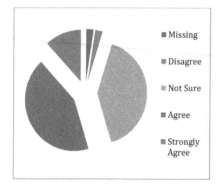

Figure 4.10 Frequency distribution pie chart of respondent on hospital readiness to adopt the e-prescription

The Table 4.19 and Fig. 4.10 represents a frequency distribution table and pie chart that shows the frequency distribution of the respondents in relating to hospital readiness to adopt e-prescription, in which out of 42 questionnaires distributed frequency of 1 and percentage 2.38% was left unfilled which represent Missing, respondents that Disagree and are Not Sure with frequencies of 1 and 17 and percentages of 2.38% and 40.48%,respondents that Agreed and Strongly Agree with the frequencies of 18 and 5 and percentages of 42.86% and 11.90% respectively.

Table 4.20 Frequency distribution table of respondent on patient readiness to adopt e-prescription

Patient ready to adopt	Frequency	Percentage of patient ready to adopt
Missing	1	2.3810
Disagree	3	7.1429
Not sure	20	47.6190
Agree	15	35.7143
Strongly agree	3	7.1429

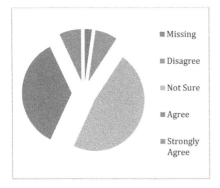

Figure 4.11 Frequency distribution pie chart of respondent on patient readiness to adopt e-prescription

Table 4.20 and Fig. 4.11 represents a frequency distribution table and pie chart that shows the frequency distribution of the respondents in relating to patient if they are ready to adopt e-prescription (organizational), in which out of 42 questionnaires distributed frequency of 1 and percentage 2.38% was left unfilled which represent Missing, respondents that Disagree and are Not Sure with frequency of 3 and 20 and percentage of 7.14% and 47.61%, respondents that Agreed and Strongly Agree with the frequencies of 15 and 3 and percentages of 35.71% and 7.14% respectively.

Table 4.21 Average mean score table

	Mean Score
Economic_ internet affordability	4.39
Economic_ paper error	4.12
Economic_ hospital affordability computer for physician	3.76
Economic_ calling time	3.48
Economic_ EP improve service quality	4.56
Economic_ save time	4.32
Economic_ EP effectiveness	3.58
Technical_ work accuracy	4.39
Technical_ internet network availability	3.41
Technical_ operating computer	4.25
Technical_ response to training	4.44
Technical_ ease of use	3.80
Technical_ motivation towards EP	4.15
Technical _ ability to use the EP	4.32
Organizational_ government response	2.46
Organizational_ Learning of computer	4.34
Organizational_ adaptation of EP	3.95
Organizational_ management of new system	3.41
Organizational_ infrastructural facilities	3.66
Organizational_ patient adaptation	3.43
Valid N	42

Table 4.21 represent a mean table that shows the average mean score of the respondents on each question in the questionnaire category Economical feasibility, Technical feasibility, and Organizational feasibility. It is the sum of each corresponding questions of the respondents divided by the total number of questions analyzed.

Table 4.22Correlation table

Correlations		Economic Feasibility	Technical Feasibility	Organizatio nal Feasibility
Economic Feasibility	Pearson Correlation	1	.174	.334*
	Sig. (2-tailed)		.311	.047
	N	37	36	36
Technical Feasibility	Pearson Correlation	.174	1	.398*
	Sig. (2-tailed)	.311		.013
	N	36	40	38
Organizational Feasibility	Pearson Correlation	.334*	.398*	1
	Sig. (2-tailed)	.047	.013	
	N	36	38	39

*. Correlation is significant at the 0.05 level (2-tailed).

Table 4.22 shows the existent and nature of correlation that exist among the three factors economic feasibility, technical feasibility, and organizational feasibility. From the table 4.22 result it appears that economic feasibility of E-prescription and technical feasibility are not correlated since p-value sig., (0.311 > 0.05 level of significant), economic feasibility and

39

organizational feasibility are correlate since p-value sig., (0.047 < 0.05) implies significant, and technical feasibility and organizational feasibility are correlate since p-value sig., (0.013 < 0.05)

4.3 RESPONDENTS

Respondents include 25 doctors, 15 pharmacists, 5 nurses, and 5 medical practitioners. Data collected on respondent profile characteristics included gender, profession, region, age, and years in practice. The majority of respondents were male (69.05%) with female making up (30.95%) of the population. Regions reported included Abeokuta (42.86%) and Lagos (57.14%) where the greater part of the respondents was attributed to the latter. Most respondents were between the age of 31-40years (50.0%), follow by 0-30years (35.71%) and with only 14.29% falling into the age category of "40 years or older". The majority of respondents had been in practice for 10-15years (42.86%), follow by less than 5year (38.10%) and only 14.29% within 16-20years of experience.

4.4ECONOMICFEASIBILITY

On the individual part, results attest that e-prescription system implementation is economically feasible since from chi-square test of the hypothesis p.value is 0.031 < 0.05 (level of significant). The EP system was reported to have a significant potential in reducing paper, time, error, and call costs leading to economic savings in medical practice. The scale means for the Likert scale based economic factors are as follows: internet affordability, 4.39; paper error, 4.12; hospital affordability computer for physician, 3.76; calling time, 3.48; e-prescription improve service quality, 4.56; save time, 4.32. On average, the economic factors were computed to have a scale mean of 4.04. Regardless of the economic feasibility on the individual basis, the Nigerian government must be willing to invest and accommodate the resources necessary for successful implementation. On the individual side, EP system implementation is economically feasible. On the government side, adequate funding does not exist for such an achievement.

4.5 TECHNICAL FEASIBILITY

Based on the feasibility analysis, results show that the higher group of respondents (85.71%) belonged to the younger age population of under the age of 40. In return, they have scored high in computer literacy (52.38%), which implies computer exposure prior to their medical practice. As suggested by Morton & Wiedenbeck (2010), "this could be reflective of the age of the majority of the respondents. It is likely that younger respondents obtained formal computer training prior to attending medical school, such as in an undergraduate program or in elementary or high school". All of the respondents use the computer regularly with 53.66% having been exposed to a healthcare system through past usage, training, and demo. This is satisfying since the majority is aware of the system's existence. The scale mean for Internet network in hospital is 3.41 portraying a level of neutrality and a slight level of satisfaction. Regardless of the stakeholder readiness; in order to reach technical readiness, Nigerian government must implement an electronic centralized medical record system. Currently, Nigerian lacks a centralized database in which patients medical records should be retained for easier diagnosis and treatment. The existence of such a central system is essential since it helps doctors and pharmacists to be on the same network, communicate through a single database, monitor patient's medical records, and share medical feedbacks.

4.6 ORGANIZATIONAL FEASIBILITY

The overall level of organizational satisfaction to e-prescription was positive since from chi-square test of the significant hypothesis test p.value is 0.032 < 0.05 (level of significant). The means fell between 3 and 4, for all factors except government respond to need of the hospital with a mean of 2.46. This scale mean shows that government-hospital relationship is very poor. Accordingly, respondents disagreed revealing their certainty that government do not respond to hospital needs. Scale means for other factors are along these lines: government response, 2.46; Learning of computer, 4.34; adaptation of e-prescription, 3.95; infrastructural facilities, 3.66 and patient adaptation, 3.43.

CHAPTER FIVE

CONCLUSION AND RECOMMENDATION

5.1 Conclusion

From the result of the analysis and interpretation in the previous chapter (four); it shows that EP system implementation is economically feasible on the side of an individual but on government side adequate funding for the achievement of EP system does not provide for the health sector to acquire the necessary resource and training skill. Regardless of the stakeholder readiness; in order to reach technical readiness, Nigerian government should implement an electronic centralized medical record system. Currently, Nigerian lacks a centralized database in which patients medical records should be retained for easier diagnosis and treatment. The existence of such a central system is essential since it helps doctors and pharmacists to be on the same network, communicate through a single database, monitor patient's medical records, and share medical feedbacks. According to the scale mean response of the respondents (2.46) shows disagreed, that reveal the certainty that government do not respond to hospital needs.

5.2 Recommendation

Nigerian government should implement an electronic centralized medical record system. Currently, Nigerian lacks a centralized database in which patients medical records should be retained for easier diagnosis and treatment. Base on the data gotten from the questionnaire we are able to identify factors that could affect the adoption of electronic prescription readiness in the southwest part of Nigeria then we recommend that more questionnaire that would cover a wider location should be designed in order to get more factors on whether Nigeria and similar third world countries are ready for the adoption of electronic prescription or not.

References

Ardava, E, Onzevs, O, Viksne, O., and Namatevs, I, (2010), Empowerment of electronic prescription for Latvian individual pharmacies with innovation initiation. Available at http://www.ism.lt/bmra/2010/CP%2050%20Ivars%20Namatevs.pdf .(accessed 29th July, 2013)

Ash, J.S., Bates, W.D., (2005). Factors and Forces Affecting HER System Adoption: Report of a 2004 ACMI Discussion. J Am Med Inform Assoc. 12:8-12.

Bell, D.S., Cretin, S., Marken, R.S (2004). A Conceptual Framework for Evaluating Outpatient Electronic Prescribing Systems Based on Their Functional Capabilities. J Am Med Inform Assoc. 11:60-70.

eHealth Initiative.(2008). A Clinician's Guide to Electronic Prescribing available at www.ama-assn.org/go/hit.(accessed 5th May 2013)

HR Policy Association. (2005).Congress Moving on Bills to Improve Health Care System Through Expanded Information Technology available at http://www.digstar.com/HR+Policy+Association (accessed 10th May 2013)

Morton M.E, Wiedenbeck, S. (2010). EHR Acceptance Factors in Ambulatory Care: A Survey of Physician Perceptions. Perspectives in Health Information Management;7:1c. Published in online research journal Available at http://europepmc.org/abstract/MED/20697466 (accessed 7th May 2013)

Perdikouri, K., Katharaki, M., (2011). Implementing and Evaluating an E-prescribing System in Greece: Findings and Recommendation. 11:203-213

Petropoulou, S.G.,Bekako, M.P., Gravvanis, G.A., (2005). E-prescribing-Telepharmacy available at http//www.aueb.gr/pympe/heremal/proceedings2005/ho5-full-papers-1/petropolou-bekakos-Telepharmarcy-pdf

RxHub. (2008). Blueprint for E-prescribing: A Detailed Plan of Action for Implementing E-prescribing available at www.surescripts.com_e-prescribing_paper_-_final_-_6.16.08.pdf(accessed 10th May 2013)

Shams, M,.(2011). Implementation of an E-prescribing Service: User's Satisfaction and Recommendations. Can pharm; 144:186-191

Stranges, E., Ryan, K., Elixhauser, A. (2008). STATISTICAL BRIEF # 104: Medicaid Hospitalizations, 2008. Available at http://www.hcup-us.ahrq.gov/reports/statbriefs/sb104.pdf (accessed 30th July 2013)

Tamblyn, R, Huang, A, Kawasum, Y, Batlett, G, GRAD, R, Jaques, A, Dawea, M, Abrahamowicz, M, Perreault, R, Taylor, L, Winslade, N,Poissant, L, Pinsonneault, A, (2006).

The Development and Evaluation of an Integrated Electronic Prescribing and Drug Management System for Primary Care. J Am med Inform assoc.13:148-159.

Speaker E. L., Audet A. J, (2006). Adoption of E-prescription Technology. Available at http://hpm.org/us/c7/4.pdf (accessed 7th May 2013)

Tan, W.T.,Phang, J.S., Tan, K.L., (2009).Evaluating User Satisfaction with an Electronic Prescription System in a Primary Care Group. Ann Acad Med Singapore 38:494-500.

Went, K., Antoniewicz, P.,Corner D.A, Dailly, S, Gregor, P, Joss, J, McIntyre, F.B, Mcleod, S, Ricketts I.W, Shearer, A.J, (2008) , Reducing prescribing errors: can a well designed electronic system help available at www.ncbi.nlm.nih.gov/m/pubmed/20102435 (accessed 14th May 2013)

Woan S. T, Jonathan S.K P., Lay K, T. (2009). Evaluating User Satisfaction with an Electronic Prescription System in a Primary Care Group. Annal Acadademy of Medicine ,38:494-500

www.ingramcontent.com/pod-product-compliance
Lightning Source LLC
La Vergne TN
LVHW092354060326
832902LV00008B/1026